FOOTBALL ATLAS

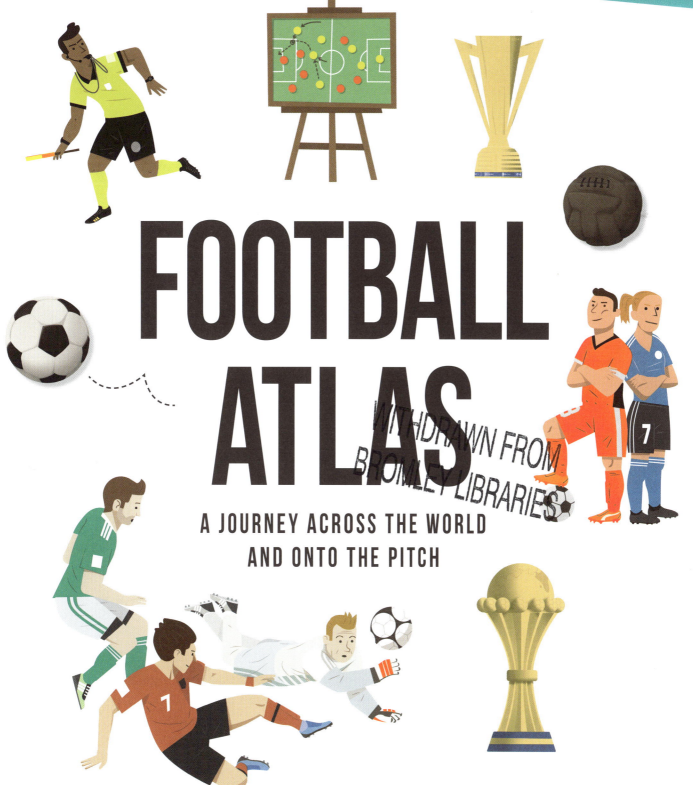

A JOURNEY ACROSS THE WORLD AND ONTO THE PITCH

James Buckley Jr.

Illustrated by Eduard Altarriba

QED

Quarto is the authority on a wide range of topics.

Quarto educates, entertains and enriches the lives of our readers—enthusiasts and lovers of hands-on living.

www.quartoknows.com

Author: James Buckley Jr.
Illustrator: Eduard Altarriba
Editor: Emily Pither
Designer: Sarah Andrews

First published in 2021 by QED Publishing,
an imprint of The Quarto Group.
The Old Brewery, 6 Blundell Street,
London, N7 9BH, United Kingdom
T: +44 (0)20 7700 6700 | F: +44 (0)20 7700 8066
www.quartoknows.com

A catalogue record for this book is available from the British Library.

ISBN: 978-0-7112-6564-6

Manufactured in Slovenia GPS042021
9 8 7 6 5 4 3 2 1

PICTURE CREDITS

-3 MAY 2023

To renew, find us online at:
https://capitadiscovery.co.uk/bromley

Please note: Items from the adult library
may also accrue overdue charges when
borrowed on children's tickets.

CONTENTS

Hi, football fans! Are you ready for a global sports adventure? Settle back in a comfy chair and I'll help you find your way to the ends of the football Earth!

PLAY FOOTBALL!

You can't go anywhere on this big, bouncing ball we call Earth without finding someone who loves football! It's the world's most popular sport and is played everywhere. It's a pretty simple game – use anything except your hands and arms to move a ball around a pitch and into a goal. It's easy to start playing, too; all you need is a ball. In this book, we'll meet a lot of football superstars from past and present, and find out where they started on this big football globe – and where they play now!

HOW TO SAY IT!

Most of the world calls this sport football. It's called soccer in the United States and Canada and a few other places. But every language has its own word. Here's how to ask for a game around the world!

"Futbol"	Spanish
"Calcio"	Italian
"Nogomet"	Croatian
"Jalkapallo"	Finnish
"Pel-droed"	Welsh
"Chuggu"	Korean
"Kurat alqadam"	Arabic
"Mpira wa miguu"	Swahili
"Whutapaoro"	Maori
"Zuqiu"	Chinese (Mandarin)

TWO WAYS TO PLAY

The top professionals play most of the time for club teams. Club teams pay their players (often, a lot!) and join leagues in each country. Players can travel far from their native countries to play for a club. Meanwhile, top players also play for their national teams, which face off against other countries. For example, Alex Morgan is a star for Tottenham Hotspurs in the English Women's Super League. She's also a key player for the United States National Team. And Neymar Jr. wears his yellow jersey for Brazil, but plays club football in France for Paris Saint-Germain.

USA national team kit

Tottenham kit

Paris Saint-Germain kit

Brazilian national team kit

A WORLD OF FOOTBALL

Games like football were first played more than 2,000 years ago. The rules may have been different from today's game, but the basic idea was much the same – to play a game of skill and teamwork. Let's kick off by travelling the globe and following the story of how football began across the world.

EUROPE

At least 2,300 years ago, the ancient Greeks played *episkyros*, a ball game with teams of 12 to 14 people. Using the hands was allowed, and so was whacking the other team!

ASIA

Cuju (see page 26) was an ancient Chinese sport played over 2,200 years ago. It is thought by some to have been the earliest form of football.

OCEANIA

Centuries before the arrival of Europeans, Aboriginal Australians and South Pacific islanders were playing team ball games. In Australia, *marngrook* was played using a coconut as a ball.

NORTH AMERICA

Native Americans enjoyed *pasuckaukohowog*, which means 'they gather to play ball with the foot'. There were up to 500 players on each side.

AFRICA

Pictures of ancient Egyptians playing ball games have been found on the walls of tombs and temples. Balls were made out of linen or cat gut wrapped in leather.

CENTRAL AND SOUTH AMERICA

Ancient people such as the Olmecs, Inca and Maya played ball games on specially built stone courts. It is thought that the losers were condemned to death!

ANTARCTICA

The first football match played in Antarctica was in 1914, during an expedition led by explorer Sir Ernest Shackleton.

THE PITCH

At every level of play, football players need a pitch! The pros play on huge areas as much as 110 metres long by 70 metres wide. Younger teams might play on smaller pitches. Most pitches are grass, but some stadiums use artificial turf. Football players love their game, though, and they'll play on just about anything – concrete, dirt, sand, asphalt and even snow!

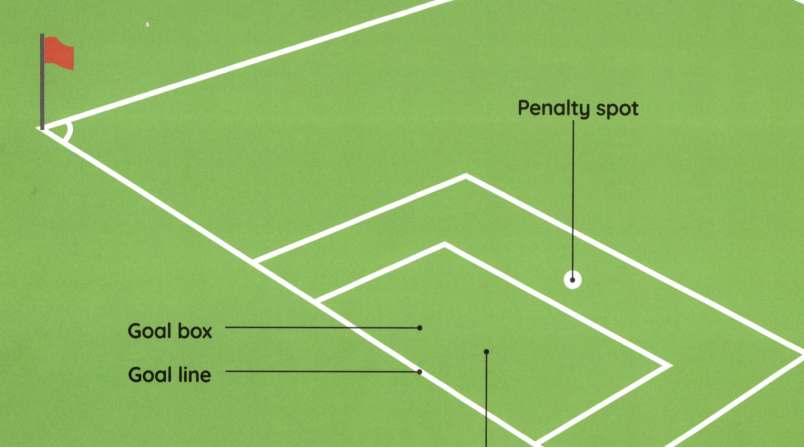

Touchline

Penalty spot

Goal box

Goal line

THE PENALTY AREA

16.5 metres out from each goal is a large box called the penalty area. These are the most important parts of the pitch, and most of the key action in the game happens in them. The lines that form the box also show the area in which the goalie can use their hands. If a major foul is called on the defence inside this area, the attacking team gets a penalty kick. That's a shot against only the goalie from the penalty spot.

THE OFFSIDE RULE

A player is caught offside if he's nearer to the opponent's goal than both the ball and the second-to-last opponent (including the goalkeeper) when his teammate plays the ball to him. In other words, a player can't receive the ball from a teammate unless there are at least two players either level with him or between him and the goal or unless his teammate plays the ball backwards to him.

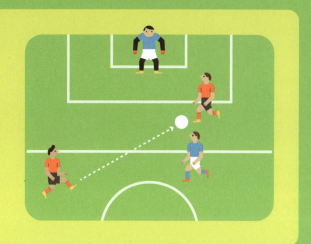

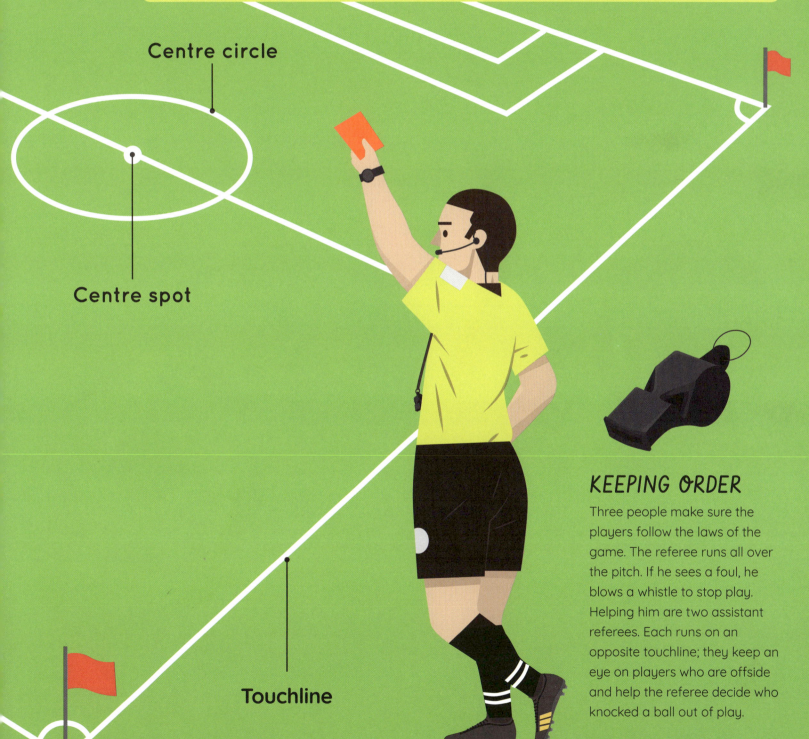

Centre circle

Centre spot

Touchline

KEEPING ORDER

Three people make sure the players follow the laws of the game. The referee runs all over the pitch. If he sees a foul, he blows a whistle to stop play. Helping him are two assistant referees. Each runs on an opposite touchline; they keep an eye on players who are offside and help the referee decide who knocked a ball out of play.

FOLLOW THE BOUNCING BALL!

Football is one of the simplest sports to play. All you need is a ball! People have been kicking around balls of all sorts for thousands of years. But when the game of football started becoming more organised, a 'real' ball was needed. Here's a look at how footballs have changed over the years. Scientists around the world are still working to make the perfect ball!

1850

Early footballs were made by covering an animal bladder with cloth or leather. But in the 1850s, rubber started being used for the first time and was a major step forwards.

1930

Better leather and tighter stitching helped improve footballs as the 20th century moved along. Balls were made in lighter colours to make them easier to see for fans and players. The number of panels varied from six to 18.

1880

By the 1880s, football size was part of FIFA rules: 68 to 70 centimetres around. Leather panels were stitched together to cover a rubber centre filled with air. However, the stitches were on the outside – they affected how the ball flew... and it hurt when you headed the laces!

1970

Inventor Buckminster Fuller inspired the most famous football design. Designers used his ideas to make a ball made up of 20 white hexagons and 12 black pentagons. Arranged the right way, they form a sphere. The Bucky Ball debuted in the 1970 World Cup and is now seen around the world.

2020

The experiments continue! Every year, ball designers try out new arrangements of shapes, colours, panels and patterns. This 2020 Premier League Nike ball has dozens of small grooves cut into the panels.

2010

The biggest change to footballs since the creation of rubber was the use of computer design and heat pressing. Instead of stitched leather panels, balls began to be made by pressing leather panels onto cloth that surrounded the rubber core. Designers also experimented with different ways to arrange the panels.

2006

For the 2010 World Cup, designers went too far! The Jabulani had eight panels of different sizes. Its surface was also given a rougher texture. Many players were not fans – they said the ball moved oddly in flight.

2014

In 2014, the ball had only six panels. The Brazuca was very popular and can still be seen in games around the world.

STADIUMS

Football stadiums around the world have become famous for their size, their style, or the historic games that have been played there. Today, the world's top teams play at state-of-the-art stadiums with undersoil heating and covered seating for tens of thousands of fans. Let's take a tour around the world and visit some stand-out stadiums.

LOCATION, LOCATION, LOCATION

Some grounds around the globe have been built in rather unusual locations...

- Built on a platform in the Marina Reservoir, the Marina Bay Stadium in Singapore is a spectacular steel structure. It can hold 9,000 fans.

- Portugal's Braga Municipal Stadium is solid as a rock. This 30,000-seat stadium was carved into the rock of a quarry at one end.

- Spare a thought for Yeovil Town FC in England – their former ground, Huish Park, had a sloping pitch. Some people said that the corner flag was level with the crossbar!

AZTECA STADIUM

Location: Mexico City, Mexico
Capacity: 87,000
Opened: 1966

THE MARACANÃ

Location: Rio de Janeiro, Brazil
Capacity: 175,000
Opened: 1950

WEMBLEY STADIUM

Location: London, England
Capacity: 90,000
Opened: 1923

RUNGRADO MAY DAY STADIUM

Location: Pyongyang, North Korea
Capacity: 114,000
Opened: 1989

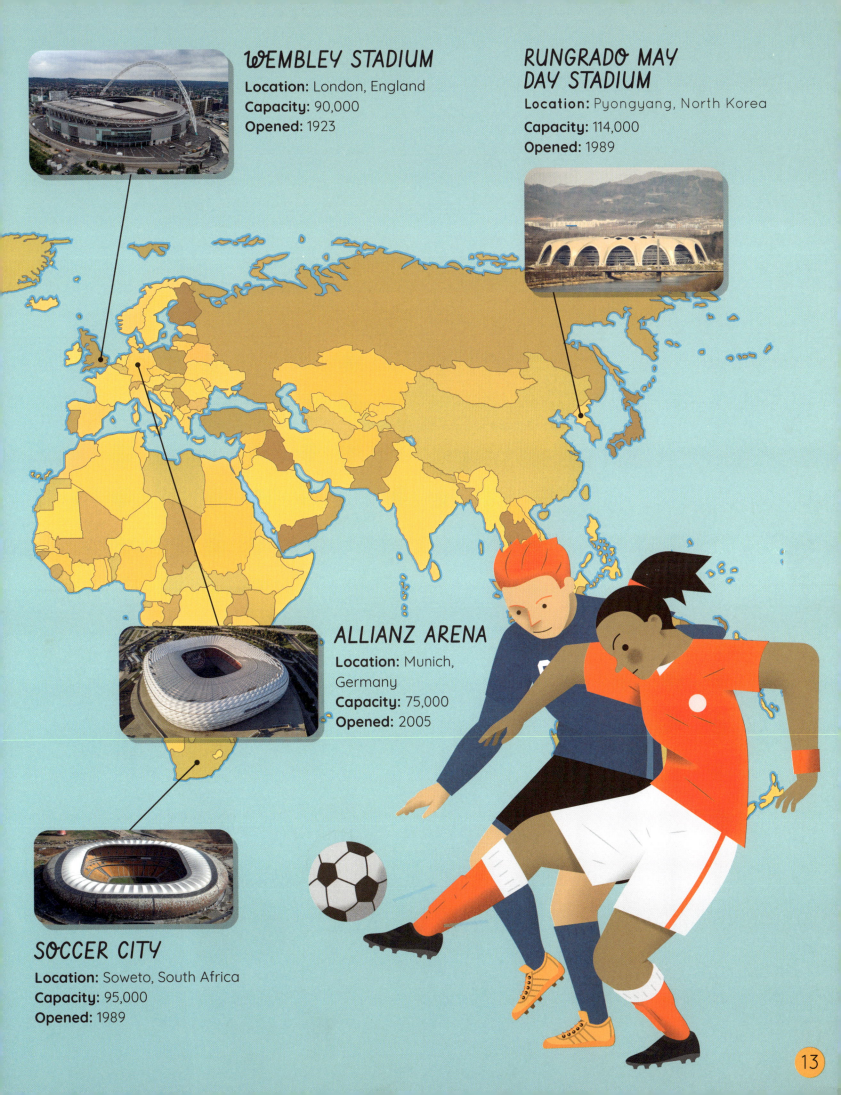

ALLIANZ ARENA

Location: Munich, Germany
Capacity: 75,000
Opened: 2005

SOCCER CITY

Location: Soweto, South Africa
Capacity: 95,000
Opened: 1989

FIFA

Football around the world is organised by the Fédération de Internationale de Football Association – known as FIFA. The French words translate to the International Federation of Association* Football. FIFA was formed in 1904 as the sport was rapidly becoming popular. A group was needed to schedule international matches and create tournaments for national teams. FIFA also became the last word on the laws of the game, so that everyone is playing by the same rules! Each country's national football association belongs to FIFA. As of 2020, 209 countries on every continent except Antarctica were members.

FIFA MEMBERS

Here's a map of the world showing the countries that are currently members of FIFA.

FIFA'S FIRST

This group of seven countries in Europe created FIFA in 1904.

SWEDEN

DENMARK

NETHERLANDS

BELGIUM

FRANCE

SPAIN

SWITZERLAND

FIFA HQ

FIFA's home is in Geneva, Switzerland. That small nation in Europe is neutral – it does not take part in wars. It's the ideal place to put FIFA so that one country is not favoured.

KEY

- FIFA members
- Non-members

*Association Football is what the game was first called in the 1800s to avoid confusion with rugby football and other early forms of similar games. In America, the sport is called 'soccer' because 'assoc.' is short for 'association'!

HERE'S HOW TO SAY IT OUT LOUD: "FEE-fah!"

LET US IN!

FIFA actually has more members than the United Nations – 209 to 196. Here are seven countries that are in the UN but are not part of FIFA... yet!

- Kiribati
- Marshall Islands
- Micronesia
- Monaco
- Nauru
- Palau
- Tuvalu
- Vatican City

FIFA'S BIG EVENTS

- Men's World Cup
- Women's World Cup
- U-20 and U-17 World Cups (M/W)
- Beach Soccer World Cup
- Futsal World Cup (indoor football)
- Olympic Football (M/W)
- FIFA Confederations Cup
- FIFA Club World Cup

CONFEDERATIONS

With every country in the world playing football, the sport needs a lot of organisation. FIFA handles the worldwide events. Below FIFA, each continental area also has its own group, called a confederation. They organise events among the member nations and plan the World Cup qualifying events. Most confederation work is for the national teams, but some pro club events are part of confederation planning, too.

UEFA

UNION OF EUROPEAN FOOTBALL ASSOCIATIONS

FOUNDED: 1954

MEMBERS: 55

FAST FACT: UEFA puts on the most popular tournaments; the confederation earned more than £1.4 billion from TV in 2019.

CONMEBOL

SOUTH AMERICAN FOOTBALL CONFEDERATION

FOUNDED: 1916

MEMBERS: 10

FAST FACT: CONMEBOL is the world's oldest football confederation.

AFC

ASIAN FOOTBALL CONFEDERATION

FOUNDED: 1954

MEMBERS: 47

FAST FACT: Surprisingly, Australia moved over from Oceania to join the AFC in 2006.

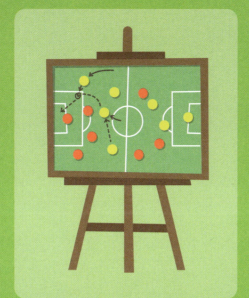

OFC

OCEANIA FOOTBALL
CONFEDERATION

FOUNDED: 1966

MEMBERS: 14

FAST FACT: The largest member nation is New Zealand.

CAF

CONFEDERATION OF
AFRICAN FOOTBALL

FOUNDED: 1957

MEMBERS: 56

FAST FACT: Three CAF teams have reached the World Cup quarter-finals: Cameroon, Senegal and Ghana.

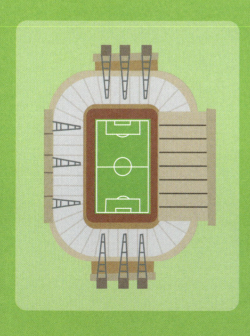

CONCACAF

CONFEDERATION OF NORTH, CENTRAL AMERICA AND CARIBBEAN ASSOCIATION FOOTBALL

FOUNDED: 1961

MEMBERS: 41

FAST FACT: CONCACAF has no Men's World Cup titles, but four Women's World Cup championships (all by the United States).

CONTINENTAL CUPS

Each confederation holds events that determine the top national teams in their region. The teams play over the course of several months, with players taking time away from their pro clubs. Most of these tournaments are not played each year. For example, the European Championship happens every four years. Playing for your country doesn't pay as much, but for players, it often means more. There's nothing quite like earning the right to wear your national colours and represent your town, state, family and nation.

GOLD CUP

CONCACAF

FIRST PLAYED: 1963

ALL-TIME MEN'S CHAMPS: Mexico (11)

ALL-TIME WOMEN'S CHAMPS (SINCE 1991) United States (8)

FAST FACT: Before the Gold Cup, each smaller part of CONMEBOL (North America, Caribbean, Central America) held its own regional championship. The CONMEBOL championship was renamed the Gold Cup in 1991.

COPA AMÉRICA

CONMEBOL

FIRST PLAYED: 1916

ALL-TIME MEN'S CHAMPS: Uruguay (15)

ALL-TIME WOMEN'S CHAMPS (SINCE 1991) Brazil (7)

FAST FACT: Argentina is the only country other than Brazil to win the Copa América Femenina, as it's known in Spanish; Argentina's win came in 2006. The men's tournament took its current name in 1975.

OFC NATIONS CUP
OFC

FIRST PLAYED: 1973

ALL-TIME MEN'S CHAMPS:
New Zealand (5)

ALL-TIME WOMEN'S CHAMPS:
New Zealand (6)

FAST FACT: In 2012, Tahiti became the only country other than Australia and New Zealand to win the men's trophy.

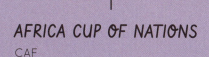

AFRICA CUP OF NATIONS
CAF

FIRST PLAYED: 1957

ALL-TIME MEN'S CHAMPS:
Egypt (7)

**ALL-TIME WOMEN'S CHAMPS
(SINCE 1991):** Nigeria (11)

FAST FACT: Two-time winner Congo (1968 and 1972) is the smallest nation to win the African Cup of Nations for men.

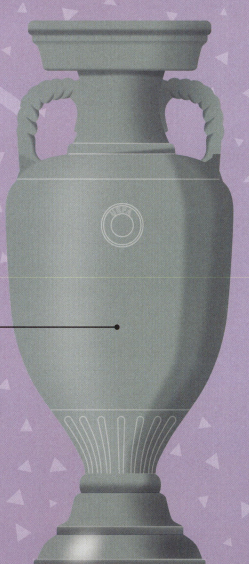

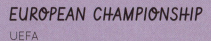

EUROPEAN CHAMPIONSHIP
UEFA

FIRST PLAYED: 1960

ALL-TIME MEN'S CHAMPS:
Germany and Spain (3)

ALL-TIME WOMEN'S CHAMPS
Germany (8)

FAST FACT: Originally called the European Nations' Cup, this popular tournament is now known by all as 'the Euros'.

THE MEN'S WORLD CUP

The FIFA World Cup is one of the biggest sporting competitions on the planet. Every four years one nation is crowned the greatest in the world after a tournament usually held in June and July. More than 200 national men's teams enter the qualifying rounds, but only the top 32 make it to the final tournament.

FIRST TIMERS

The first official World Cup was held in 1930 in Uruguay. Only thirteen countries competed as organisers struggled to persuade teams to travel to South America. In the final, Uruguay defeated Argentina 4–2 and became the first nation to win the World Cup.

WINNERS

Although football is a global game, only eight different nations have won the World Cup. The hosts of the competition (as well as the winners of the last competition) qualify automatically for the final stages of the tournament.

COUNTRY	WINS	TOURNAMENT YEAR
Brazil	5	1958, 1962, 1970, 1994, 2002
Italy	4	1934, 1938, 1982, 2006
Germany	4	1954, 1974, 1990, 2014
Uruguay	2	1930, 1950
Argentina	2	1978, 1986
France	2	1998, 2018
England	1	1966
Spain	1	2010

TROPHY TROUBLE

The first World Cup trophy, the Jules Rimet Trophy, was stolen just weeks before the 1966 World Cup in London, England but was found by a dog named Pickles. His reward was a year's supply of dog food. The trophy was given to Brazil permanently after it won the World Cup for the third time in 1970 but was again stolen in 1983 and has never been found. The current trophy, designed by Italian artist Silvio Gazzaniga, has been used since 1974 and is made of 18-carat gold.

SCORING RECORDS

- England's Geoff Hurst is the only man to score three goals in a World Cup final. His hat-trick helped the host nation beat West Germany 4–2 at Wembley in 1966.

- The first ever World Cup hat-trick was scored by the USA's Bert Patenaude, in a 3–0 victory over Paraguay in 1930.

- Oleg Salenko scored a World Cup record five goals in one game, when Russia beat Cameroon 6–1 in 1994.

HOSTING THE WORLD CUP

Putting on the World Cup is a huge deal. Dozens of teams and millions of fans pour into the host nation to watch the games. In the group stage, each team plays three games. Then the knockout rounds are played until only two teams are left standing. The World Cup final is one of the most popular sporting events on the planet. It's usually played in the host nation's biggest city.

HOW MANY TEAMS?

Year(s)	No. Teams
1930	13
1934-1978	16*
1982-1994	24
1998-2022	32
2026	48

*The 1950 event had only 15 teams.

MAP SHOWING WORLD CUP HOSTS

Canada
(2026)

United States
(1994, 2026*)
*Scheduled
as of 2021.

Brazil
(1950, 2014)

Mexico
(1970, 1986, 2026*)
*Scheduled
as of 2021.

Chile
(1962)

Argentina
(1978)

Uruguay
(1930)

FOOTBALL IN THE DESERT

Qatar will host the World Cup in 2022, and the whole football world is waiting to see what it will be like. Qatar is located on the Arabian peninsula, and can be very hot. To avoid the heat, this World Cup will be in November and December instead of the usual summer dates. In Qatar, seven stadiums are being built from scratch to host the games. Most have air-conditioning, even though most are all outside! The largest, in Lusail, will seat more than 80,000 for the final.

England
(1966)

Sweden
(1958)

West
Germany
(1974, 2006)

Japan
(2002)

Switzerland
(1954)

Russia
(2018)

South Korea
(2002)

Italy
(1934, 1990)

Qatar
(2022)

France
(1938, 1998)

Spain
(1982)

South Africa
(2010)

Lusail Stadium, Qatar

THE WOMEN'S WORLD CUP

While the Men's World Cup started back in 1930, FIFA did not start a Women's World Cup until 1991! What took them so long, right? From only 12 teams in the first event, the Women's World Cup had grown to 24 teams by 2019. And more than 140 nations compete in qualifying tournaments to reach that final 24. Women's football has grown thick and fast in the past two decades.

ALL-TIME CHAMPIONS AND RUNNERS-UP

YEAR	CHAMPION	RUNNER-UP
2019	United States	Netherlands
2015	United States	Japan
2011	Japan	United States
2007	Germany	Brazil
2003	Germany	Sweden
1999	United States	China
1995	Norway	Germany
1991	United States	Norway

MEMORABLE MOMENTS

- Women's football took a huge leap forwards at the 1999 World Cup. The biggest TV audiences yet saw a great tournament. The US beat China in a penalty shoot-out. Brandi Chastain's famous celebration was seen around the world!

- Germany made it two in a row with a big win over Brazil in 2007. Megastar Birgit Prinz scored the opening goal of her team's 2-0 victory.

- Homare Sawa of Japan scored with just three minutes left in extra time to tie with the US. Japan then shocked the Americans with a win in penalty kicks for its first world championship.

- The US won its fourth World Cup in 2015 when Carli Lloyd had a hat-trick in the first fifteen minutes of the final. One of her goals was from more than 45 metres out!

FINAL DESTINATIONS

Here's where the Women's World Cup finals have taken place.

2015 CANADA

2011 GERMANY
2019 FRANCE

1995 SWEDEN

1991 CHINA
2007 CHINA

2003 USA

1999 USA

2023* AUSTRALIA

*Scheduled as of 2021

25

FOOTBALL IN ASIA

Football is one of the fastest-growing sports in many Asian countries. Qatar, the host of the World Cup in 2022, is included in the enormous Asian Football Confederation, whose members stretch from Lebanon in the west to Japan in the east. Most of the larger nations have pro football leagues, with China's being the biggest. Women's football is growing even faster than men's in some nations. While no Asian men's team has made a World Cup final match, Japan won the 2011 Women's World Cup. China's women's team is also one of the best in the world. Among men's teams, Iran is usually the highest ranked.

A BILLION EYES

English Premier League games get huge ratings in places like China, Japan and India. Fan clubs for the big teams can be found in large cities. Some studies say that more than a billion people watch Premier League games in Asia; that is far and away the biggest audience of any region of the world! How can you tell? Look at the shirts of EPL teams and see how many are sponsored by Asian companies.

WORLD CUP SHOCKER!

At the 2018 Men's World Cup, the South Korean team shocked the football world. They faced mighty Germany in the final game of the group stage. Germany needed to win to advance; South Korea was already out. But in the 96th minute, South Korean star Son Heung-Min (page 28) scored to give his team the stunning victory and send the Germans packing!

FAST FACT

Similar to football, *cuju* was an individual or team-based foot-and-ball game. It is thought that the sport was probably officiated by a referee, and was played for fun, as well as for military training.

South Korea **2 - 0** Germany

TOP LEAGUES

These are the biggest pro leagues in Asia.

NATION	LEAGUE	FOUNDED	TEAMS	FAST FACT
Japan	J-League	1992	18	– The Kashima Antlers have won a record 8 J-League titles.
China	Chinese Super League	2004	16	– Brazilian stars like Oscar help make Chinese teams 'super'
South Korea	K-League	1983	12	– Players from Europe and all over Asia play in the K-League.

SUPERSTARS OF ASIA

Asia has not produced as many world superstars as Europe or South America... but that is changing. Players from China, Japan, Korea and other Asian nations are now seen more often in top leagues around the world. Here are some greats from past and present.

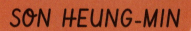

ALI DAEI

IRAN

No male player has scored as many international goals as Ali Daei's 109, though Canada's Christine Sinclair and several other women have topped that mark. Daei played for Iran's national team from 1993 to 2006.

SON HEUNG-MIN

SOUTH KOREA

An exciting, high-scoring star for Tottenham in the Premier League, Son Heung-Min has won three Best Asian Footballer awards. He helped South Korea reach the World Cup in 2014 and 2018.

SUN WEN

CHINA

Named the co-Player of the Year for the 20th century among women, Sun Wen won Golden Ball and Golden Shoe trophies at the 1999 World Cup. She scored 106 career goals for China and helped win a 1996 Olympic silver medal.

HOMARE SAWA

JAPAN

Her 205 caps are the most ever for a Japanese player. She was also the first player from Asia to be named FIFA Player of the Year (2011). She led Japan to a surprise 2011 World Cup title and helped them finish second in 2015.

CHA BUM-KUN

SOUTH KOREA

Few Asian football players had made an impact in Europe before Cha Bum-kun started in Germany in 1978. In 12 seasons, he became a top scorer, putting in more than 40 goals for two different clubs.

FOOTBALL IN AFRICA

Football arrived in Africa with the European colonists. They brought a lot of troubles to Africa, but football was not one of them! The sport has spread across the continent and is now number-one in just about every African nation. Most of the teams do not have nearly as much money as European or North American clubs, but players from Africa can be found on top clubs around the world. With a growing population and excited fans, Africa will be a big part of football's future.

PIONEERING HEROES

Eusébio grew up in Mozambique. His talent on the pitch took him to Portugal, where he became one of the best players in the world in the 1960s. He helped Benfica win 11 league titles and he led all of Europe in scoring twice. In 1965, he became the first player from Africa named as the top pro player in Europe. His success inspired many African players to try to make it big in world football.

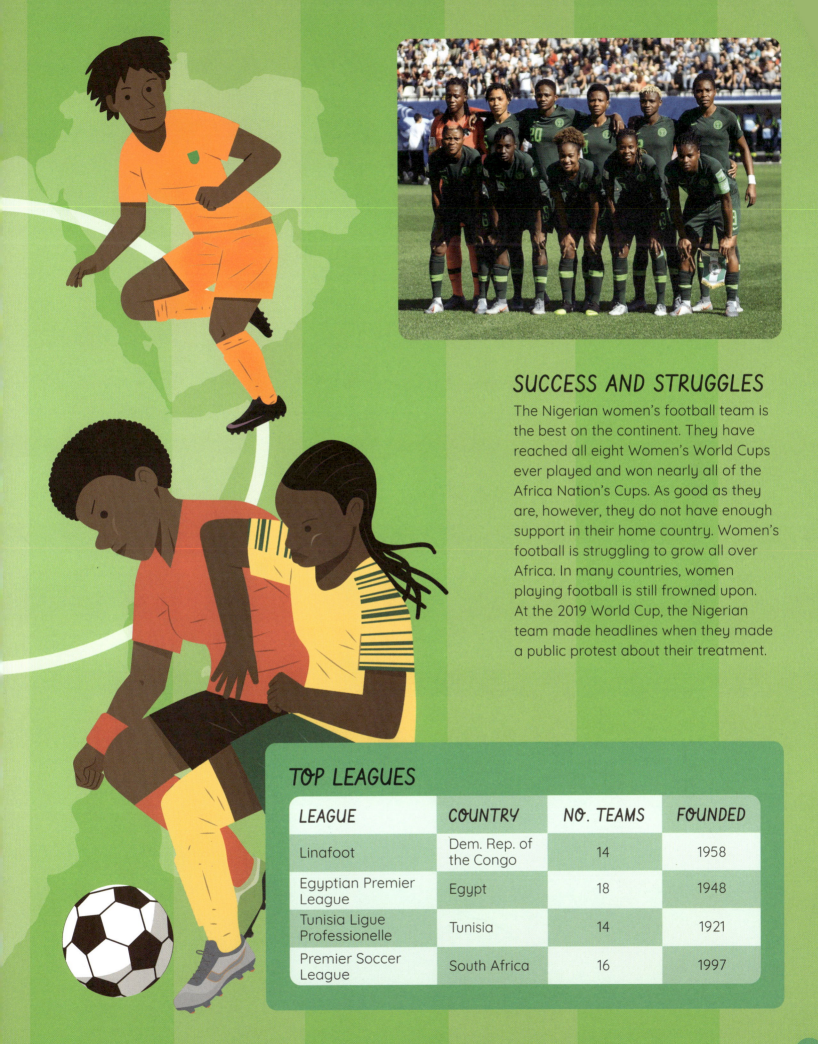

SUCCESS AND STRUGGLES

The Nigerian women's football team is the best on the continent. They have reached all eight Women's World Cups ever played and won nearly all of the Africa Nation's Cups. As good as they are, however, they do not have enough support in their home country. Women's football is struggling to grow all over Africa. In many countries, women playing football is still frowned upon. At the 2019 World Cup, the Nigerian team made headlines when they made a public protest about their treatment.

TOP LEAGUES

LEAGUE	COUNTRY	NO. TEAMS	FOUNDED
Linafoot	Dem. Rep. of the Congo	14	1958
Egyptian Premier League	Egypt	18	1948
Tunisia Ligue Professionelle	Tunisia	14	1921
Premier Soccer League	South Africa	16	1997

SUPERSTARS OF AFRICA

H ere are some of the best players from yesterday and today who come from countries in Africa.

GEORGE WEAH

LIBERIA

The only player from Africa to win the Balon D'Or (1995) as the top player in the world, Weah was a high-scoring forward. He scored 57 goals with Monaco. He moved to Paris-St. Germain and became an international star as they earned a league title. He moved to AC Milan and won two more league championships. Weah ended up with more goals in Europe than any other African player. After his playing career ended, he entered politics. Weah is now the president of Liberia.

ASISAT OSHOLA

NIGERIA

Only 26, Oshola already has three African Player of the Year awards and was the BBC Women's Footballer of the Year in 2015. For Nigeria, she was the top scorer at the U-20 World Cup and helped her country win two Africa Cups. After playing in Nigeria and England, she joined Barcelona and quickly became its top scorer.

ROGER MILLA

CAMEROON

Leading the Indomitable Lions of Cameroon, Milla became a World Cup legend with his play in 1990. He played again in 1994 when he was 42, the oldest World Cup player ever! He scored more than 400 goals and was African Player of the Year twice.

DIDIER DROGBA

IVORY COAST

Drogba had a nose for the goal, scoring more than 300 times for Chelsea. He helped the Blues win four league titles and four FA Cups. His penalty-kick goal gave his team the Champions League title in 2012. He was twice named African Player of the Year.

SAMUEL ETO'O

CAMEROON

Few players on any continent have as many awards and trophies as this all-round star. He earned four trophies as the top player in Africa, helped Cameroon win the 2000 Olympic gold medal, and was a Champions League winner with Barcelona and Milan.

TABITHA CHAWINGA

MALAWI

She might single-handedly lift Malawi to success in Africa. As a pro, she has been a goal-scoring machine, including 123 in three seasons in Sweden. Moving to China, she led its pro league with 17 goals in her first season! She's a rising star to watch!

FOOTBALL IN EUROPE

Football was born in Europe in the 1800s and it remains the world centre of the sport today. At the professional club level, football is organised by the Union of European Football Associations (UEFA; usually pronounced "yoo-WAY-fah"). UEFA was formed in 1954 by Italy, Belgium and France. Most countries have several levels of club football, from the most elite top levels down to smaller, local clubs. Each league crowns an annual champion based on league games played. Leagues also each hold an annual 'Cup' tournament, a knockout event that often includes teams at many levels.

MOVING UP AND MOVING DOWN

Almost every football league in Europe (and many on other continents) uses a system called 'relegation and promotion'. Each season, a set number of teams at the bottom of the standings move down one level (relegation). The same number move up a level (promotion). This can mean a huge change in a team's fortunes. In 2020, Fulham returned from the Football League Championship to the Premier League. The move earned Fulham more than 160 million pounds in TV money. That's a lot of new footballs and kit!

THE BIG FIVE

Every member of UEFA in Europe has its own professional league except for one country: Liechtenstein. These are the biggest and most popular leagues in Europe. The top teams in all UEFA leagues take part in the Champions League (see page 40).

LEAGUE	COUNTRY	NO. TEAMS	FOUNDED
Premier League	England	20	1992*
Serie A	Italy	20	1898
Bundesliga	Germany	18	1962
La Liga	Spain	20	1929
Ligue 1	France	20	1932

*This replaced the top division of football in England that had actually started way back in 1863!

SUPERSTARS OF EUROPE

There's a whole world of football superstars from Europe! With so many players and so many countries to choose from, every fan has their favourites! But here is a selection of just a few football legends from the past and present.

FRANZ BECKENBAUER

GERMANY

You know you're good if you remake how the game is played. 'Der Kaiser', as he was known, was the first great sweeper. He turned defence into offence and paved the way for players to roam the pitch and score. As a star with Bayern Munich, he was twice the world Player of the Year. He also captained West Germany to the 1974 World Cup title and three European Cup wins. Later, he helped put the US on the football map with a stint on the famous New York Cosmos. Then he became the German national team coach and in 1990 was the first player-coach champ!

PAOLO MALDINI

ITALY

Perhaps Italy's greatest player ever was this goal-stopping defender. Maldini played more games in Italy's Serie A than any other player. While Maldini was anchoring AC Milan, the club won 25 trophies in all competitions, including five Champions Leagues and seven Serie A titles.

JOHANN CRUYFF

NETHERLANDS

If you play, then you've probably tried the move named for this Dutch superstar. The 'Cruyff Turn' means passing the ball behind one of your feet to change directions quickly. Cruyff's all-round skills helped make Dutch 'Total Football' a huge success in the 1970s.

KELLY SMITH

ENGLAND

Few players, men or women, had a nose for the goal like this striker. With 46 career goals, she remains England's all-time leading scorer among women, and she helped Arsenal win four Premier League titles. Her scoring skills helped the Lionesses reach two World Cups, too.

DAVID BECKHAM

ENGLAND

'Becks' did one thing better than just about anyone: free kicks. His ability to bend and swerve the ball into the goal made him a legend. He made his name with Manchester United and later Real Madrid. In 2007, he moved to the LA Galaxy and helped make that US league a success.

BIRGIT PRINZ

GERMANY

Some put her on top of the list of the best European players ever. After joining the German team at only 16, she was a star for the next 17 years. Germany won four European titles with Prinz as forward. They also won a pair of Women's World Cups (2004 and 2007). Prinz was the FIFA Player of the Year three times (2003-05).

ZINIDINE ZIDANE

FRANCE

This French star was the best wherever he went. He was the Player of the Year in French, Italian, and Spanish leagues, as well as a four-time world Player of the Year. Tall, strong, and powerful, he was a tough opponent even for the best. His high point came in 1998 when he led his country to the World Cup title at home in Paris.

TODAY'S STARS: EUROPE

Most of the top players from Europe have stayed home to play on European clubs. But they are always ready to leap into action for their national teams, too!

KEVIN DE BRUYNE
MANCHESTER CITY

The heart of Manchester City's speedy offence is this passing machine from Belgium. He helped City set a points record in 2018 and then tied a Premier League record in 2019–20 with 20 assists.

CRISTIANO RONALDO
JUVENTUS

Since Ronaldo joined Manchester United in 2003, Portugal's five-time world Player of the Year has captured the world's attention. With Manchester United, he won two Premier League Player of the Year awards and helped his team win the Champions League. In 2009, Ronaldo moved to Real Madrid and led them to four Champions League trophies; he also became the career leader in Champions League goals. Now with Juventus in Italy, he has scored more than 700 goals for club and country.

HARRY KANE
TOTTENHAM HOTSPUR

A three-time Premier League top goalscorer, his 39 goals in 2017–18 set a new league record. His precision shooting also helped Spurs reach the 2018 Champions League final and put England into the 2018 World Cup semi-finals.

LUCY BRONZE
MANCHESTER CITY

Bronze's solid defence almost turned into gold for England at the 2019 Women's World Cup and helped her earn Women's Player of the Year. She starred for Olympique Lyonnais before coming home to England in 2020.

ROBERT LEWANDOWSKI
BAYERN MUNICH

Few players score as often as this Polish striker. He has helped his German club win eight Bundesliga titles. Lewandowski was named FIFA Player of the Year for 2020.

KYLIAN MBAPPÉ
PARIS-ST. GERMAIN

This speedy scoring star thrilled fans at the 2018 World Cup and has helped his team become a league champion. The forward's thrilling dribbling runs have made him a superstar-in-the-making.

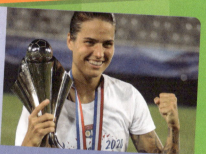

DZENIFER MAROZSÁN
OLYMPIQUE LYONNAIS

With a European championship and Germany's first Olympic gold medal in football, midfielder Marozsán leaped into the elite of women's players. She scores goals as well as setting up teammates and shows her leadership as the German team captain.

LIEKE MARTENS
FC BARCELONA FEMENI

Martens was the 2017 World Player of the Year and has helped the Netherlands win a European title. A high-scoring winger, she had big goals on the way to her nation's runner-up spot at the 2019 World Cup.

LUKA MODRIĆ
REAL MADRID

Modrić teamed with Ronaldo on Real Madrid and now feeds passes to stars like Eden Hazard and Karim Benzema. He helped Croatia reach the 2018 World Cup final.

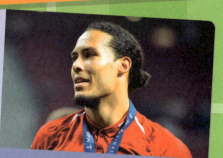

VIRGIL VAN DIJK
LIVERPOOL

Perhaps the best defender in the world, the big Dutchman helped Liverpool win its first Premier League title in 2020.

UEFA CHAMPIONS LEAGUE

In club football, how do you decide who is the best of the best? Each league crowns a champion, of course, but what if you got all those champs together to see who is REALLY number one? That's the idea behind the UEFA Champions League, formerly known as the European Cup when it started in 1955. Each year, the top 32 teams from among the leagues in UEFA enter into a months-long tournament. After playing in small groups, the top 16 teams enter a thrilling play-off series. The winners meet in the Champions League final, one of the most-watched sports events each year.

WOMEN'S CHAMPIONS LEAGUE

Spain has dominated the Men's Champions League but in the women's version, first played in 2002, a team from France are the queens. Olympique Lyons has won seven Women's Champions League titles, including five in a row from 2016-20. FFC Frankfurt has won four, the last being in 2015.

BETTER THAN SECOND BEST

Another continent-wide tournament brings in great clubs that did not quite make it into the Champions League. Since 1958, the Europa League has gathered teams from all over Europe. It's a great way for fans to see clubs from all over take on their favourites – if the clubs are lucky enough to make it in! FC Sevilla from Spain has six Europa titles and six clubs are tied for second with three each.

SHOW THEM THE MONEY!

To players and fans, the Champions League is probably just a notch below the World Cup. It's the second-biggest prize in football. For the winning team, it's also a huge pile of money! In 2020, the winning teams could have earned more than £70 million for their wins and the championship. But it's the winner's medal that means the most.

ALL-TIME CHAMPS

These are the teams that have won the most Champions League/European Cup titles.

CLUB	TITLES	MOST RECENT
Real Madrid	13	2018
AC Milan	7	2007
Bayern Munich	6	2020
Liverpool	6	2019
Barcelona	5	2015

FOOTBALL IN NORTH AMERICA

In North America, there are two stories of football (or soccer as it's known there). In Mexico, the sport is number one. Liga MX features the top 18 clubs, but more than 60 other pro teams play below them. In the United States and Canada, however, women's football has led the way. Those two national teams are among the best in the world, with the US winning a record four Women's World Cups and Canada often among the top-ranked. Women's pro football leagues, however, have not been as successful. Meanwhile, the top American men's pro league, Major League Soccer, is growing fast. In 2021, it will play its 26th season and welcome its 30th team.

YOUTH FOOTBALL

A huge reason for the growth of football in the United States in the 2000s is youth football. Unlike in many other countries, thousands of American kids play in organised leagues. They learn the game early and become fans and players as they grow up. More than two million children play on youth teams in the US.

PELÉ LED THE WAY

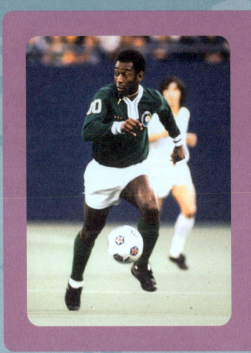

In 1975, Brazilian superstar Pelé (page 50) joined the old North American Soccer League. Though he only played for three years, he started a parade of top European and South American players who have come to the US, often towards the end of their careers. Major League Soccer has benefited from all those transfers – here are just a few of the superstars who have helped it grow and pulled in fans who have watched their heroes for years.

- David Beckham, England and LA Galaxy
- Thierry Henry, France and NY Red Bulls
- Zlatan Ibrahimović, Sweden and LA Galaxy
- Kaká, Brazil and Orlando City
- Wayne Rooney, England and DC United

HIGH SCHOOL AND COLLEGE FOOTBALL

In most countries, football is played by athletic clubs. They organise all the teams at all age levels. In the United States, club football is growing, but high school and university (college) football is where most young players take to the pitch. High school teams play each other in leagues and play-offs. College teams travel around the country to match up against schools of similar size. The annual College Cup is the biggest event on the college football calendar.

SUPERSTARS OF NORTH AMERICA

Most of the all-time heroes in US football have been women, as the nation has produced way more top female stars than male stars. In Mexico, the list of choices for heroes is much longer – but are mostly men. In Canada, their best player is still playing; you'll meet her on the next page!

MIA HAMM

USA

Until she was topped by teammate Abby Wambach, this striker's 158 international goals were the most ever – man or woman. Mia Hamm first gained notice while helping North Carolina begin a football dynasty; she was a four-time national champ with the Tar Heels, who have won 21 titles overall. At 15, Hamm helped America win its first World Cup in 1991. She repeated the feat in 1999 and also won Olympic gold medals in 1996 and 2004.

LANDON DONOVAN

USA

Though current star Christian Pulisic might give him a run for his money, at the moment, Donovan is the best overall men's player in US history. He played for a time in England and Germany but he made his biggest mark in Major League Soccer. He won four titles with the LA Galaxy and one with the San Jose Earthquakes. He was also part of three US World Cup teams.

MICHELLE AKERS

USA

Joining Mia Hamm as a women's football pioneer, Akers paved the way for American success as part of the first national team ever and scorer of the country's first international goal in 1985. She was the top scorer among all players as the US won its first World Cup in 1991; she helped win a second in 1999 as the team's veteran leader. She shared the award as the FIFA Player of the Twentieth Century with China's Sun Wen.

ABBY WAMBACH

USA

Wambach's height and leaping ability made her a goal-scoring machine for the US team. Her 184 international goals are second-most of all time behind Canada's Christine Sinclair (page 46) but still first among Americans. Wambach was the 2012 world Player of the Year, and was a part of four World Cup teams, earning a champion's medal in 2015.

HUGO SÁNCHEZ

MEXICO

Named the top North American player of the 20th century, this Mexican goal-scoring machine helped Real Madrid dominate Spanish football during his more than 280 games with them. He led La Liga in scoring four times and helped Madrid win five league titles. In his best seasons, he scored 157 goals in only four years! He also helped 'El Tri' reach three World Cups.

RAFA MÁRQUEZ

MEXICO

For more than 20 years, one thing was certain for Mexico's national team: Rafa Márquez was the defensive anchor. He is one of only three players ever to appear in five World Cups for his country. He helped Mexico win a pair of Gold Cups, and starred in leagues in Mexico, the United States, France and Greece.

TODAY'S STARS: NORTH AMERICA

More and more top international stars are making their mark from North America. Americans and Canadians play in leagues around the world. In 2020, a record seven played in Champions League games. Meet North America's top players!

TIM HOWARD

This veteran goalkeeper has anchored the 2010 and 2014 US World Cup teams. He has played more international games than any other US keeper. His 16-save performance in a 2018 loss to Belgium is an all-time classic. Howard started more than 400 games in the Premier League and now plays for a USL team of which he is part-owner!

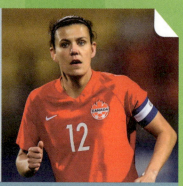

CHRISTINE SINCLAIR

Who is the all-time leader in goals scored for a national team? Not Ronaldo, not Messi, not even Pelé. One player stands atop that important list: forward Christine Sinclair of Canada. Through 2020, she has scored 186 goals in her maple-leaf shirt. Sinclair has helped Canada reach five World Cups; she became the second woman ever to score in five Cups, too. Sinclair has a pair of Olympic bronze medals and has been named Canada's Player of the Year an incredible 14 times. Since 2013, she has played for the Portland Thorns of the National Women's Soccer League (NWSL) in the USA.

CHRISTIAN PULISIC

If this speedy young midfielder keeps it up, he might overtake Landon Donovan as the best American player ever. Pulisic moved to Europe at 16 to start his pro career, and he soon was starring for Borussia Dortmund in Germany. He moved to Chelsea in 2020 and became an impact player. He is the clear leader of the young US national team, too.

ALEX MORGAN

Morgan is a scoring machine with more than 100 goals for the US national team. She helped the Americans win the 2015 and 2019 Women's World Cups and the 2012 Olympic gold medal. Fast and talented on the ball, her nose for the goal has also helped several pro teams in the US; she also won a Champions League title with Lyon in France in 2017.

CARLI LLOYD

Lloyd's favourite number must be two: that's how many World Player of the Year awards, World Cup titles and Olympic gold medals she has. Her hat-trick in the 2015 World Cup final – in 15 minutes! – was an all-time football highlight. She has been part of several pro teams in the US, most recently for Sky Blue FC.

MEGAN RAPINOE

Few athletes in any sport have had the worldwide impact that Megan Rapinoe had in 2019. While leading the US to the Women's World Cup and earning the tournament MVP award, 'Pinoe' also became a world spokesman for gender equality. Her free-kick abilities helped her win the World Player of the Year award in 2019.

CARLOS VELA

This Mexican star was the MLS MVP in 2019, when he also set a new league record with 34 goals for LAFC. He used to play in Spain and England, and has made more than 70 starts for Mexico. His left foot is one of the world's most accurate!

FOOTBALL IN SOUTH AMERICA

This continent is home to the nation with the most World Cup championships. Brazil has been best in the world five times; you can count the stars its players wear on their uniforms! Brazil is also home to what some people call the best-ever men's and women's players of all time – Marta (page 52) and Pelé (page 50). Argentina is home to the oldest league in the world outside England. Football is No. 1 in every other South American country, too, drawing huge crowds of fans.

BRAZIL

WOMEN'S FOOTBALL IN SOUTH AMERICA

This continent is further behind in making sure women can play top-level football. Brazil has a very strong women's team and a pro league, but Argentina only allowed pro football for women in 2019. Eight other South American countries don't even have leagues yet. Brazil has made the Women's World Cup eight times (and finished second in 2007), but the other South American nations have combined for only eight appearances all together.

Maracanã Stadium, Rio de Janeiro

CENTRAL AMERICAN FOOTBALL

The nations of Central America are part of CONCACAF. However, they nearly all speak Spanish and are closer in culture to the countries of South America. Costa Rica has had the most success among Central American countries. Los Ticos, as they are known, have reached five World Cups. In 2018, they made it to the round of 8, tied for the best finish by a Central American team.

TOP LEAGUES

NATION	COUNTRY	TEAMS	FOUNDED
Primera División	Argentina	24	1891
Campeonato Brasilieiro Série A	Brazil	20	1959
Primera A	Colombia	20	1948

SUPERSTARS OF SOUTH AMERICA

There are enough superstars from Brazil and Argentina to fill this whole book, but here are some superstar highlights from a range of countries in South America.

PELÉ

BRAZIL

Though he grew up playing without shoes in Brazil, Pelé left the football world as the greatest player of all time. He helped Brazil win three World Cups and played a huge part in football's global growth. Pele played his last game in 1977 for two teams – in the first half, he played for Santos. In the second, he put on the Cosmos shirt for the final time.

DIEGO MARADONA

ARGENTINA

Some people think that Maradona was better than Pelé. Though short and stocky, Maradona was fast and fierce. His dribbling runs were incredible and his nose for the goal unstoppable. He led Argentina to the 1986 World Cup title, where he was named the Golden Ball winner as top player. His play was legendary.

RONALDO

BRAZIL

After Pelé, this high-scoring striker was perhaps Brazil's best. He is second all-time in World Cup goals with 15 and earned a championship with Brazil in 1994. He was a three-time world Player of the Year and a goal-scoring star with Inter Milan in Italy and Real Madrid in Spain. If not for knee injuries, he might have topped all the records.

CARLOS VALDERRAMA

COLOMBIA

Valderrama's amazing hair made him easy to spot on any pitch. His incredible passing also made him stand out. Valderrama earned more caps for Colombia than any other player, and was named the top player on the continent three times. After playing in Colombia and Spain, he became one of the top players in Major League Soccer.

ALFREDO DISTÉFANO

ARGENTINA

In the 1950s, no one was better than DiStéfano. As the leader of Real Madrid, one of the greatest club teams of all time, this super dribbler helped his team win five straight European Cups. He scored in five straight Cup finals, including a hat-trick in 1956. He played internationally for Spain and for his native Argentina.

TEÓFILO CUBILLAS

PERU

Probably the greatest player in Peruvian history, midfielder Cubillas is one of only three players to score in five different World Cups. He led Peru to the 1975 Copa America title, too. He played pro football in Peru and in the United States.

GARRINCHA

BRAZIL

Dribbling is a key part of football, and some experts think this Brazilian star was the best ever. He was a key part of Brazil's 1958 and 1962 World Cup wins; he was the top player of the 1962 tournament. He played his whole club career with Botafogo in Brazil.

ELÍAS FIGUEROA

CHILE

Defenders don't get as much attention as high-scoring forwards, but this centre back is probably Chile's greatest player ever. He led his country to three World Cups and starred for clubs in Chile, Brazil and Uruguay. Figueroa was named the continent's top player three times.

TODAY'S STARS: SOUTH AMERICA

South American countries have sent some of football's most legendary players to the world stage. The tradition continues – two of the very best players in the world are from South America, along with many others in the top ranks.

MARTA
BRAZIL

Experts agree: this goal-scoring forward is one of the best women's football players of all time. A five-time World Cup team member for Brazil, she has won six world Player of the Year awards, the most ever –man or woman. Her 17 World Cup goals are the most ever – again, man or woman. As a pro player, she has starred in leagues in Sweden, Brazil and the United States.

LIONEL MESSI
ARGENTINA

Football fans split into two groups. One group says Cristiano Ronaldo is the greatest player alive. The other group says it's this high-scoring Argentinian forward. Nicknamed 'The Flea', Messi is small but just about unstoppable on the dribble. Messi is about speed, style and surprise. He moved from his home to play for Barcelona when he was just 13. He made the first team four years later and has become the greatest scorer in La Liga history; he also has more goals than any other player from football-mad Argentina. He's a five-time winner of the Balon D'or as the world's best player. His 91 goals in 2012 are the most ever in a single year. Though he has not won a World Cup yet, he did lead Argentina to the 2008 Olympic gold medal.

NEYMAR JR.
BRAZIL

If not for Ronaldo and Messi, this speedy young forward might be the world's best. His greatest achievement so far was leading Brazil to the 2016 Olympic gold medal. His penalty kick in the final clinched that long-awaited goal. He's only 27 as of 2020, but he is Brazil's third-leading scorer ever! As a pro, he stars now for Paris-St. Germain after playing in Brazil and Spain.

ALISSON BECKER
BRAZIL

In 2020, this amazing goalie was the only South American player named to the FIFA World XI (the line-up of the best players). He helped Liverpool win the 2019 Champions League and 2020 Premier League titles. Tall, fast and strong, he's the No. 1 keeper!

LUIS SUÁREZ
URUGUAY

When he is not annoying opponents and making trouble, Suárez is scoring goals – more than anyone else in his country's history. With his national team, Suárez helped win a record 15th Copa America and has been part of three World Cup teams. As a pro, he led the Premier League in goals with Liverpool and earned a Champions League title with Barcelona. He plays now for Atletico Madrid in Spain.

SERGIO AGÜERO
ARGENTINA

A goal-scoring machine, he was the youngest player ever in pro Argentinian football at the age of only 15! He later moved to the Premier League team Manchester City, and has become that league's highest goal-scorer ever for a player from outside Europe. He has been part of three World Cup teams, too.

COPA LIBERTADORES

The best pro clubs in South America meet each year in this big tournament. However, unlike some other continental championships, Copa Libertadores sometimes invites outside nations – Mexico, for example, has been in several Copa Libertadores. However, South American teams have dominated. Argentine clubs have won 25 times and ten different clubs from Brazil have won at least once.

WHAT'S IN A NAME?

Most South American countries were once colonies of European nations. In the 1800s and 1900s, the people fought to free themselves and become independent. The name of the tournament translates to 'Liberators of America Cup'. It honours the men who helped to free, or liberate, their homelands.

ALL-TIME CHAMPS

CLUB	COUNTRY	TITLES
Independiente	Argentina	7
Boca Juniors	Argentina	6
Peñarol	Uruguay	5
River Plate	Argentina	4
Estudiantes	Argentina	4

WOMEN'S TOP GOAL SCORERS

Cristiane, Brazil	15	
Gloria Villamayor, Chile	8	
Noelia Cuevas, Paraguay	8	

COPA LIBERTADORES FOR WOMEN

Since 2009, top women's clubs have played for a similar title. Not surprisingly, Brazil leads the way with eight victories – São José has the most with three. Clubs from Colombia, Chile and Paraguay have one win each. Good news for the future: no men's club team can enter Copa Libertadores unless they also field a pro women's team!

FOOTBALL IN OCEANIA

Oceania is a large region in the South Pacific which includes dozens of countries, most of which are islands. The Oceania Football Confederation is the smallest of FIFA's confederations, but the sport is growing in many of its members. Australia is the largest country in the region, but it's not part of the Oceania Football Confederation any more, having 'moved' to the Asian Football Confederation in 2006. New Zealand is probably the region's top football country now.

2023, HERE WE COME!

The 2023 Women's World Cup will be played in Australia and New Zealand. The two nations will share games among the 32 international teams.

WORLD CUP APPEARANCES

Most Oceania nations are very small and can't compete with the top teams in the world. Only Australia (1974 and 2006) and New Zealand (1982 and 2010) have earned a spot at the big event. But let's give a shout-out to tiny Solomon Islands, which reached the Beach Soccer World Cup three times!

TOP LEAGUES

LEAGUE	COUNTRY	TEAMS	FOUNDED
A-League	Australia	12	2005
ASFA Soccer League	American Samoa	12	1976
New Zealand Football Championship	New Zealand	10	2004
New Caledonia Division Honneur	New Caledonia	8	1962

SUPERSTARS OF
OCEANIA

Oceania's countries have a long love of football, but have not produced nearly as many world-class players as some other regions. But some have made their marks on the international game, including these stars of yesterday and today.

CHRISTIAN KAREMBEU

NEW CALEDONIA

Since his country is a part of France, Christian Karembeu played for the French national team in more than 50 games and won the World Cup in 1998. He starred in European leagues in Italy, Spain and England, and won a pair of Champions League titles, too. He was named the top player in Oceania twice!

WYNTON RUFER

NEW ZEALAND

In 2000, writers elected this top-flight striker the Oceania player of the 20th century! Rufer is the best Kiwi player ever and spent many seasons in Germany's top league. He helped his nation reach the World Cup in 1982 as well.

TIM CAHILL

AUSTRALIA

Cahill is Australia's all-time leading scorer, with 50 goals in more than 100 games. He put in at least one goal in three World Cups. He played more than 400 games in the Premier League and also played in India, China and the USA.

HARRY KEWELL

AUSTRALIA

Injuries slowed what would have been an even greater career, but Kewell did pretty well when he played! He was the youngest Australian national team player ever at age 17. At the 2006 World Cup, his goal clinched his team a rare spot in the round of 16. He also played many years in the Premier League in England.

SAM KERR

AUSTRALIA

You must be pretty good if you're the all-time leading scorer in two pro leagues! Kerr is top in her native nation's W-League as well as the NWSL in the United States. The four-time PFA women's Player of the Year, she has helped the Aussies reach three World Cups. In 2020, she joined Chelsea in England.

OTHER WAYS TO PLAY

Football is such a popular game that people around the world have created a variety of different ways to play it. Here's a look at some popular football games that people play around the world.

FUTSAL

Football indoors? Why not! Faster paced than outdoor football, futsal uses five-player teams on a court about the size of an ice-hockey rink. The ball is a bit smaller than the outdoor ball and is made to bounce less. But players can kick the ball off walls to pass to themselves!

MOTOBALL

Talk about fast-paced! Not even Lionel Messi could keep up with the players in this sport. Motoball players wear helmets and ride motorbikes as they kick and pass a large ball. Teams from Russia have dominated most competitions.

POWERCHAIR FOOTBALL

Powerchair football players use motorised wheelchairs to move around an indoor court. Teams of four players pass and shoot the ball with bars on their chairs.

BEACH FOOTBALL

If you think running on sand is tough, try playing football on it! Countries with beaches are perfect places to play this tricky sport. Four players and a goalie play on each team. The pitches are about 35 metres long. The rules are mostly the same as regular football, but dribbling and running are much harder!

BLIND FOOTBALL

For this game, teams play in silent arenas with a ball that makes noise. Players follow the ball by sound but otherwise play like regular football.

PARTIALLY-SIGHTED FOOTBALL

Partially-sighted football is played by players with a visual impairment. The rules are based on Futsal with a small number of adaptations including reduced pitch markings, a ball colour that contrasts from the pitch and lines, and specific light requirements during a match.

GOAL!

ow that we've travelled all around the football world and back, it's time for you to get out and play. Gather your friends and teammates, then try some of these games. Football is a great sport to read and learn about... but it's even more fun to play!

PENALTY SHOOTOUT

Set up two teams of shooters. Put cones about 1 metre from each goalpost. How many shots can your team make between the cones and the post? You don't even need a goalie for this one!

KIT DESIGNER

Too cold or wet to play? No problem! Here's an inside football activity. Get some paper and pens and create your own kit design. What colours will you use? What will your team logo look like? Let your imagination run wild! And don't forget to design awesome-looking boots!

MINI WORLD CUP

Gather a group of friends and create a football tournament. You can have as many players on each team as you want. Here's the catch: each team represents a country. Where is your family from? Do you have friends with backgrounds in other nations? Set up a tournament and see which 'country' wins!

JUGGLING CONTEST

Who can keep the ball in the air for the most touches? Who can keep it in the air for the longest? The more you practise this game, the better you'll get! You can even juggle with friends in a circle – what is your all-time record for touches?

AUTHOR'S NOTE

I hope you've enjoyed this tour of the world of football. I've been playing or coaching the game for more than 40 years. I still play today in an adult football league. The players in our league in Santa Barbara, California, come from dozens of countries; it's like a World Cup every weekend! Our team captain is from Colombia, and my teammates are from Mexico, Guatemala, El Salvador, Chile, Croatia, Iran and of course America! Over the years, I've played with players from Japan, Germany, England, France, Sweden, Brazil, Uruguay, Nigeria, Ghana, Australia and even far-off Fiji, among many other countries. We didn't always share the same language, but we all spoke football! No matter where you go, you'll be able to be part of the world of football. I hope this book can be your passport to getting started! Thanks for reading!

James Buckley Jr.

Sportswriter

& Goalie (Portero), The Renegades

INDEX